No-Sweat
FLANNEL QUILTS
FAST AND FUN DESIGNS

BETH GARRETSON

Martingale®
& COMPANY

That Patchwork Place® is an imprint of
Martingale & Company®.

Martingale & Company
20205 144th Avenue NE
Woodinville, WA 98072-8478
www.martingale-pub.com

The information in this book is presented in good faith, but no warranty is given nor results guaranteed. Since Martingale & Company has no control over choice of materials or procedures, the company assumes no responsibility for the use of this information.

Printed in China
09 08 07 06 05 04   8 7 6 5 4 3 2 1

Library of Congress Cataloging-in-Publication Data

Garretson, Beth.
    No-sweat flannel quilts: fast and fun designs /
Beth Garretson.
        p. cm.
    "That Patchwork Place."
    ISBN 1-56477-540-2
1. Patchwork—Patterns. 2. Machine quilting.
3. Flannel. I. Title.
    TT835.G3695 2004
    746.46'041—dc22
                                    2004003592

Credits

President: Nancy J. Martin
CEO: Daniel J. Martin
Publisher: Jane Hamada
Editorial Director: Mary V. Green
Managing Editor: Tina Cook
Technical Editor: Karen Costello Soltys
Copy Editors: Karen Koll and Durby Peterson
Design Director: Stan Green
Illustrator: Laurel Strand
Cover and Text Designer: Shelly Garrison
Photographer: Brent Kane

Mission Statement

Dedicated to providing quality products
and service to inspire creativity.

Dedication

To my mother, Peggy Hancock,
who tried for years to convince me I could be a
teacher and a writer. Mom, you were right.

Acknowledgments

My sincere thanks to all who helped me make this
dream a reality. I am particularly grateful to

Brad and Sue McMillan, Betty Hamilton, and all my
students at Bernina Sewing Center in Yakima
who inspire me so much.

Robin Hancock, Teresa Hancock, and Kelsey
Williams for their assistance and advice.

Donna Garretson, a great friend and
the best cousin-in-law in the world!

Michaela Hughes, an extraordinary long-arm
machine quilter who graciously takes on the big
quilting jobs I don't want to tackle.

Karen Soltys, Terry Martin, and the rest of the fine
folks at Martingale & Company who helped me turn
a head full of ideas into a book worth publishing.

Most of all to my husband, Peter:
You make it all possible, dearest love.

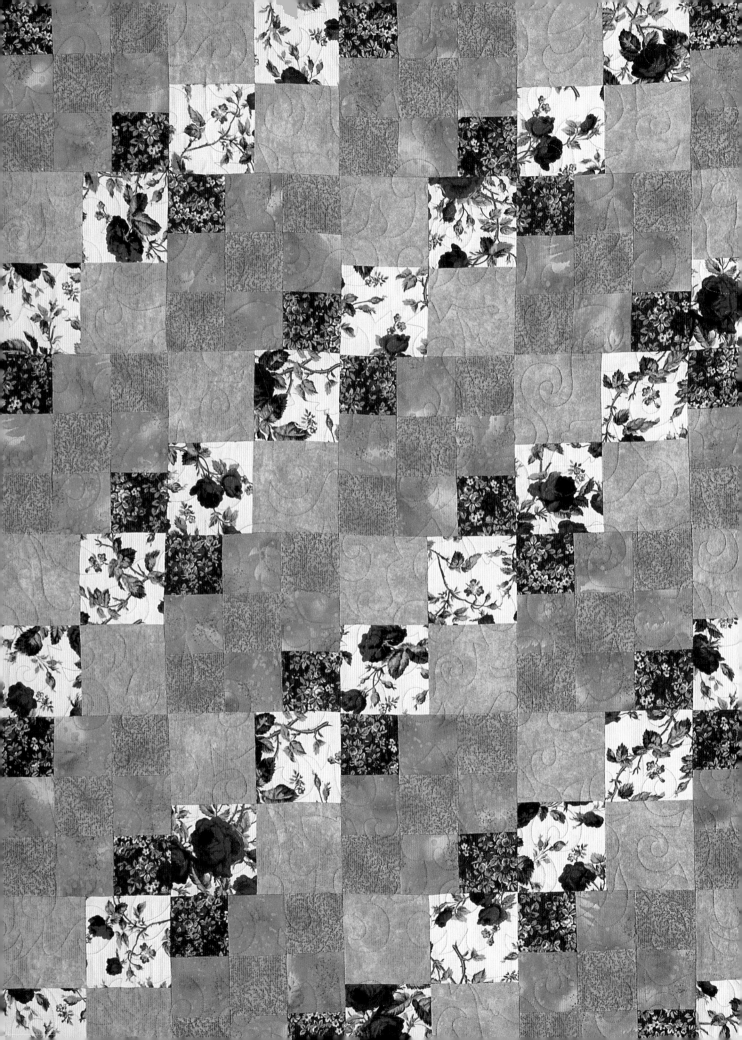

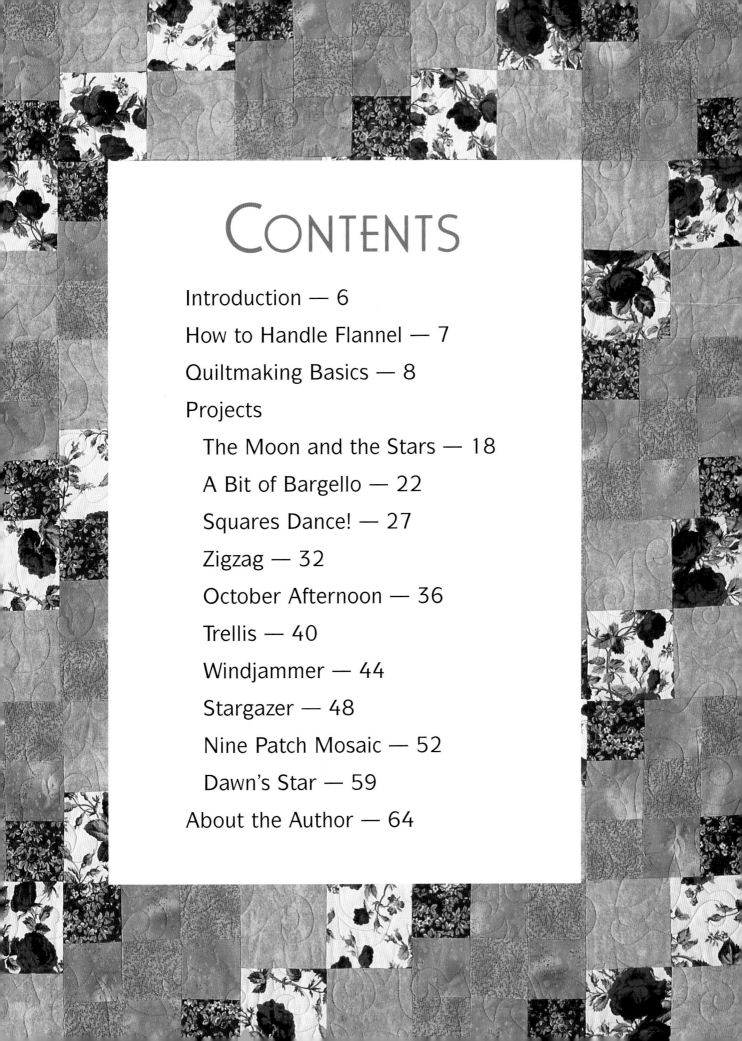

CONTENTS

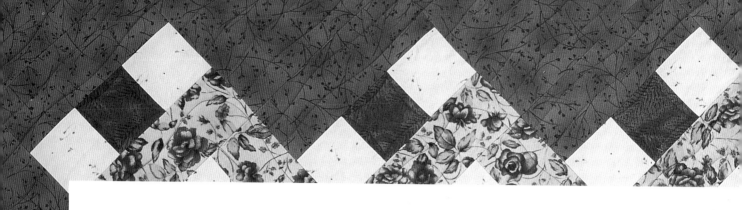

INTRODUCTION

My first experience quilting with flannel was not a happy one. I chose a block that was far too complicated and treated the fabric like any other quilting cotton. The first block was sadly misshapen and nearly an inch smaller than the desired finished size. I might have thrown in the towel if not for my part-time job at a great quilt shop. Surrounded by fabulous flannels, I decided to find a better way to make quilts with these fabrics.

In this book, you will find lively projects that sew up swiftly. There are plenty of pointers on how to use the special properties of flannel to your advantage so that your quilt will be a success. These simple yet dynamic designs are perfect for those occasions when a quick gift is needed, and a quilt is expected.

With so many beautiful flannels on the market, there has never been a better time to use these fabrics in your quilts. Dive in and have fun. Remember, it's no sweat!

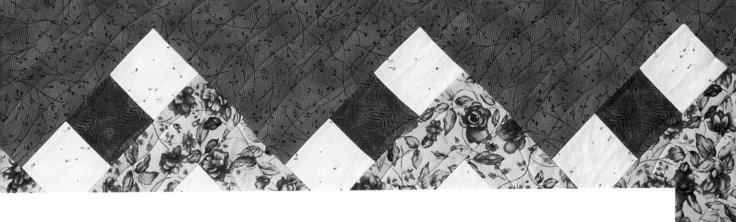

HOW TO HANDLE FLANNEL

Flannel is warm, cuddly, and fuzzy. The quality of today's flannel fabric is astonishingly higher than it was just five years ago. Even so, because of its very nature, the fabric tends to shrink and distort more than regular quilting cottons. Fortunately you need only follow a few basic "rules of the road" to ensure that your flannel experiences will be fun, not frustrating.

1. Wash and dry flannels twice before you use them. This assures you of minimal shrinkage later on and removes a lot of lint that would otherwise end up in your sewing machine.

2. Treat the fabric gently throughout the quiltmaking process. Resist the urge to push or pull the fabric into place. Instead, use a lifting motion to reposition it. The less you stretch your flannel, the more precise your results will be.

3. Place bias edges next to the feed dogs of your machine whenever possible. Bias edges are more prone to distortion than straight-grain edges, so place the straight-grain edges next to the presser foot.

4. Place "squirrelly" fabrics next to the feed dogs. Once in a while you will come across a flannel that stretches even along a straight-grain edge. I call these mischief makers "squirrelly" and treat them the same as I treat bias edges.

5. Reduce the amount of pressure on your sewing-machine foot if possible. My machine has a dial on the side that allows me to control how hard the foot pushes down on the fabric. While sewing flannel, I reduce the pressure slightly.

6. Press seams open. Please read the section on pressing in "Quiltmaking Basics" (see page 11) for an explanation of why this is such an important step.

7. Purchase generous amounts. Flannel not only shrinks more than regular quilting cotton, in some cases the width of the fabric is narrower from the start. Check this information on the bolt. In addition, your favorite print may sell out very quickly, and your quilt shop may not be able to reorder it. Better to have a bit left over than to run short!

QUILTMAKING BASICS

The following sections provide information on tools and techniques used to complete the projects in this book.

Tools

Below is a list of the essential tools you will need to complete the projects in this book. Experience has taught me that the old saying "a good tool is a joy to work with" is absolutely true. I encourage you to supply yourself with the best tools you can find.

Rotary-cutting tools: A cutter with a sharp blade is a must. I prefer the large (60 mm) cutter for flannel because it slices through thick fabric easily. Acquire a self-healing mat that is at least 24" wide in one direction. Acrylic rulers in a variety of sizes will simplify the cutting process. You will need a 6" x 24" ruler to cut strips. I also used 6" x 6", 6" x 12", and 15" x 15" rulers extensively while making the quilts for this book.

Sewing machine: A machine that produces a good straight stitch is essential for quilting success. If you plan to quilt or apply the binding to your projects by machine, you will need a walking foot. Free-motion quilting requires a darning foot and the ability to drop or cover your feed dogs. Good machine maintenance is a must! Familiarize yourself with the cleaning instructions for your machine. It is a good idea to check for lint build-up every time you change your bobbin.

Thread: Use a good-quality, medium-weight, cotton thread. Your machine will be happier and so will you! I stock up on light- to dark-gray threads for piecing cool-colored fabrics (greens and blues) and cream to brown threads for warm-colored fabrics (reds and yellows). For quilting, I'm having a lot of fun these days with the new variegated-color cotton threads.

Needles: Use a size 14/90 sewing-machine needle and change to a fresh one often. I replace my needle after emptying two bobbins of thread or after four to six hours of sewing.

Seam ripper: Find one with a small, sharp point and keep it close by. Un-sewing is not fun, but it is even more miserable with a bad tool.

Pins: Long slender pins with glass heads will hold your fabric together and not melt if you touch them with an iron.

Scissors: A small pair of scissors or snips will come in handy for clipping threads.

Marking tools: There are many tools available for marking fabric. I prefer a light marker for dark fabrics and a dark marker for light fabrics. Test your markers on scrap fabric to be sure that you will see them when you need to and that they will disappear when you want them gone.

Rotary Cutting

Rotary-cutting techniques are used throughout the projects in this book. All measurements include standard ¼" seam allowances. If you are unfamiliar with rotary cutting, read the brief introduction that follows. For more detailed information, see *Shortcuts: A Concise Guide to Rotary Cutting* by Donna Lynn Thomas (Martingale & Company, 1999). Remember to keep a fresh blade handy, as flannel will dull your blade more quickly than regular quilting cotton. Make a habit of closing the guard on your blade after every cut. It will help prevent nicks on your blade as well as unfortunate accidents.

1. Fold the fabric in half, wrong sides together, matching selvages. Align the crosswise and lengthwise grains as well as possible. There should be no wrinkles along the folded edge. Place the fabric on the cutting mat, folded edge nearest you. Align a square ruler along the folded edge of the fabric. Place a long, straight ruler to the left of the square ruler, just covering the uneven raw edges of the left side of the fabric.

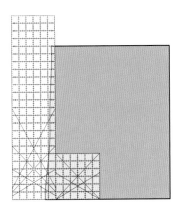

2. Carefully remove the square ruler without moving the long, straight ruler. Cut along the right edge of the long ruler, rolling the rotary cutter away from you. Discard this strip. (Reverse this procedure if you are left-handed.)

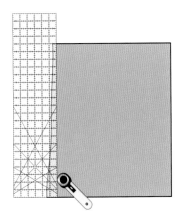

3. To cut strips across the width of the fabric, align the newly cut edge of the fabric with the ruler markings at the appropriate measurement. For example, to cut a 3"-wide strip, place the 3" ruler mark on the edge of the fabric.

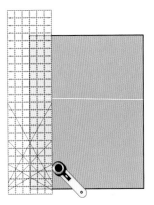

4. To cut squares or rectangles, cut strips the required width and trim the selvage edges off the strips. Align the left edge of the strips with the correct ruler marking. Cut the desired shape. Continue cutting squares or rectangles until you have the number needed.

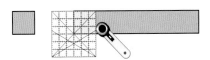

5. For half-square triangles, begin by cutting a square ⅞" larger than the desired finished size of the short side of the triangle. Then cut the square once diagonally, corner to corner. Each square yields two half-square triangles. The short sides of each triangle are on the straight grain of the fabric.

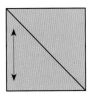
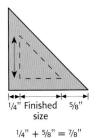

¼" Finished 5/8"
size

¼" + 5/8" = ⅞"

6. For quarter-square triangles, begin by cutting a square 1¼" larger than the desired finished size of the long edge of the triangle. Then cut the square twice diagonally, corner to corner. Each square yields four quarter-square triangles. These triangles will have the straight grain on their long side.

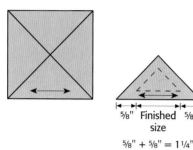

⅝" Finished ⅝"
size
⅝" + ⅝" = 1¼"

Note: For the projects in this book that have a diagonal set, I have oversized the setting triangles. This ensures that you will have a bit more than a ¼" seam allowance around the edges of the quilt. It will give you a little breathing room when you square up the quilt or apply the binding.

❧ DOUBLE LAYER ONLY! ❧

Because flannel is thicker than regular quilting cotton and more difficult to cut through, you may find it easier to fold the fabric only once (two layers) rather making a double fold (four layers) for cutting. It's much easier to distort the shape of your strips or pieces when cutting through too much fabric at once.

Seam Allowances

All of the projects in this book are designed for speedy cutting and piecing. Maintaining accuracy as you zip along will reward you with a beautiful quilt in the end. It is important to establish a true ¼"-seam allowance before you begin sewing your precisely cut pieces. I encourage you to experiment with flannel scraps until you establish an exact ¼"-seam allowance. You may be able to find a special patchwork or ¼"-foot to fit your machine. This accessory allows you to use the edge of the foot to guide the fabric and achieve a perfect ¼" seam. If this option is not available to you, create a seam guide on your machine by placing a piece of tape or moleskin or a magnetic seam guide ¼" away from the needle.

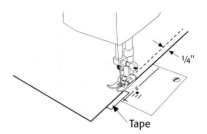

¼"

Tape

Chain Piecing

Once you have established a true ¼"-seam allowance, I invite you to try chain piecing! Chain piecing makes good use of your time and thread. The projects in this book lend themselves very well to this technique.

1. Sew a pair of pieces from cut edge to cut edge, using 12 to 15 stitches per inch. Stop sewing at the edge of your first pair but do not cut the thread.

2. Position the next pair of pieces under the presser foot, as close as possible to the first. Continue feeding pairs of pieces through the machine without cutting threads.

3. When all the pairs are sewn, remove the chain from the machine and clip the threads between the pairs of sewn pieces.

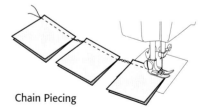

Chain Piecing

Strip Piecing

Strip piecing is a great timesaving technique. Many of the quilts in this book use this method of piecing. Read the pressing tips in the next section to ensure nice straight strip sets.

1. Sew a pair of strips from selvage edge to selvage edge, using 12 to 15 stitches per inch. Continue sewing strips to the first pair as required, until your strip set is complete. Press seams open after each addition to the strip set.

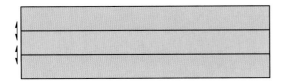

2. Trim the selvage edges from the strip set. Align the newly cut edge of the fabric with the ruler markings at the appropriate measurement and cut the required number of segments across the set. Many times this measurement will be the same as the width of the strips used in the strip set. For example, if the strips are 3" wide, you will often cut the segments 3" wide.

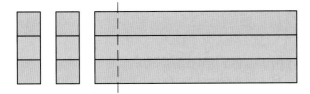

Pressing

Careful pressing is as vital to the success of your project as accurate cutting and seaming. The traditional rule in quiltmaking is to press seams to one side. Flannel, however, is more bulky than regular quilting cottons. Your blocks will have a much better chance at finishing to the correct

size if you press the seam allowances open. Here are a few pointers to help take the "pressure" off your pressing experience:

1. Press on the wrong side of the fabric. I like to rake the main portion of the fabric lightly away from the seams with the backs of my fingertips before pressing. This keeps the seam from falling over to one side.

2. The pressing motion should always be up and down. Moving the iron side to side or back and forth will quickly distort the fabric.

3. Use plenty of heat and/or steam. This will help you get a nice flat seam more quickly and reduce your inclination to use any sort of back-and-forth "scrubbing" motion with the iron. It's that motion that causes the distortion. Use the smallest amount of pressure needed to accomplish the task. Less pressure means less distortion.

4. Press long seams across the width of the ironing board rather than along the length of the board. This is particularly important when pressing seams for strip sets. I find that it is very easy to produce a curved or bowed seam if it is pressed along the length of the board. By pressing with the strips across the width of the board, you press a shorter section at a time. You have to pick up the iron and move the strip set, rather than glide the iron along the entire length. Again, it's this up and down motion (rather than the gliding or moving along the strip) that will lead to better accuracy.

5. The seam allowances for plain border strips may be pressed toward the border rather than open. At this point in the construction of your quilt, a tiny bit of extra bulk in the seam allowance will not cause a problem. Also, it's unlikely that you will be quilting on the border side of the seam, so the extra bulk there should not hinder your quilting.

Joining the Blocks

Below are two quick explanations for joining blocks to create a quilt top. The first is for straight sets and the second is for diagonal sets. Refer to the quilt layout diagram provided with each project for specific directions.

For straight-set quilts, arrange the blocks according to the project diagram. Sew blocks together in horizontal rows. Next, sew the rows together, taking care to match the seam intersections.

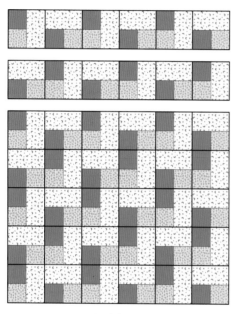

Straight Set

For diagonal-set quilts, arrange the blocks, side setting triangles, and corner triangles according to the project diagram. Sew the blocks and side setting triangles in diagonal rows. Pay particular attention to which side of the triangle should be joined to the block. It is easy to get turned around! Next, sew the rows together,

matching seams between blocks. The last step is to sew the corner triangles to the completed top. Please note that all project directions call for oversized setting triangles. After all rows are sewn together, use a long rotary-cutting ruler and a rotary cutter to trim the excess fabric.

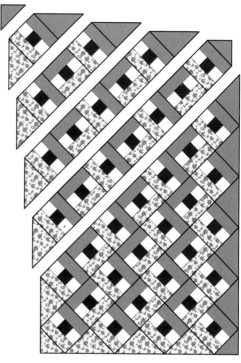

Diagonal Set

Adding Borders

Before applying borders to your quilt top, it is best to measure through the center in both directions to determine the actual size of the top. It has been my experience that flannel quilts tend to stretch or "grow" a bit. All of the borders in this book, except for those on Nine-Patch Mosaic, are done with straight strips of fabric. In most cases, you will need to cut multiple strips for each border and seam them together.

A diagonal seam requires a little more fabric but is not as noticeable as a seam that runs perpendicularly across the border. A horizontal seam uses slightly less fabric, but it tends to catch the viewer's eye. Each project including borders in this book calls for enough border strips to make diagonal seams.

With one exception, all the quilts with borders are constructed with the side borders applied first. The top and bottom borders are applied last as shown in the diagram at right. For the quilt "The Moon and the Stars," the top and bottom borders are applied first to make more economical use of the fabric. Refer to the following steps for applying straight, flat borders.

1. Measure the length of your quilt top through the center and cut two border strips to that measurement, piecing as necessary. Mark the centers of the strips and the side edges of the quilt. Pin the strips to the sides of the quilt, matching the centers and the ends first. Continue pinning, placing pins about 4" apart. Stitch the borders in place. Press seam allowances toward the borders.

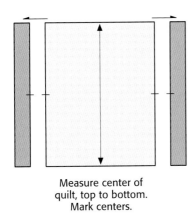

Measure center of
quilt, top to bottom.
Mark centers.

2. Next, measure the width of your quilt top through the center and cut two border strips to that measurement, piecing as necessary. Mark the centers of the strips and centers of the top and bottom of your quilt. Pin border strips as you did for the sides of the quilt, matching centers and ends first. Stitch the borders in place. Press seam allowances toward the borders.

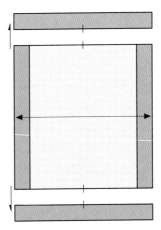

Measure center of quilt, side to
side, including border strips.
Mark centers.

You are now ready to set up your quilt for the final phase!

Preparing to Quilt

Now that your top is finished, it is time to prepare the layers for quilting. Follow the instructions for machine quilting in this section if you are planning to quilt your project at home. I do not recommend hand quilting for flannel quilts. If you wish to have your project quilted by a professional machine quilter, please consult her (or him) before you construct the back of the quilt or mark the top. I recommend using very thin cotton batting for a warm and cozy flannel quilt. My personal favorite is Quilter's Dream Cotton Request. If you use medium- to heavy-weight batting, the result may be an overly hot and oppressive quilt.

1. If you choose an intricate quilting pattern, you will need to mark it on the quilt top before you proceed to the next step. Use a marking tool that is both easy to see and easy

to remove from the fabric. I prefer to keep the quilting motifs simple on flannel quilts and avoid too much marking. I generally use masking tape to mark grids or to follow seam lines, and I occasionally use a chalk wheel or stitch-through paper to mark a design. Test your marking method on scraps from your project. If you use masking tape for marking long, straight lines, beware of leaving it on your project for any length of time. It can leave a sticky residue that may be difficult to remove.

2. Cut the backing fabric and the batting 6" larger than the quilt top. The projects in this book will require two or, in some cases, three lengths of fabric sewn together in order to reach the required size. Trim away selvage edges before piecing the lengths. After the lengths are sewn together and seams pressed open, trim away any excess fabric.

3. Lay the completed backing, right side down, on a smooth, flat surface. Secure all the edges with masking tape, pins, or clamps. The back should be smooth and wrinkle-free but not stretched. Center the batting over the backing and carefully flatten any bumps. Center the quilt top, right side up, over the backing and batting. Check the edges of all layers. They should be parallel to each other, and there should be the same amount of backing and batting showing around each edge of the quilt top. Gently smooth the top from the center to the edges until it lies flat. As with the backing, take care not to stretch the fabric.

4. Baste the layers together with rustproof safety pins. Begin in the center and work your way to the edges. Continue to smooth the top as

needed. Place pins 6" to 8" apart. As much as possible, avoid pinning directly on your quilting lines.

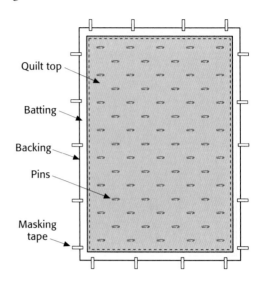

Machine Quilting

Machine quilting is appropriate for all types of quilts, and flannel quilts are no exception. In fact, as I stated earlier, I do not recommend hand quilting for these projects. They are designed for quick sewing, everyday use, and frequent laundering. For straight-line sewing you will need a walking foot. Use a darning foot and lower or cover your feed dogs for free-motion quilting. Each project in this book includes quilting suggestions. I encourage you to use them as a starting point and let your creativity guide your own quilting stitches.

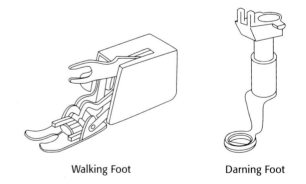

Walking Foot   Darning Foot

For more information about machine quilting see *Machine Quilting Made Easy!* by Maurine Noble (Martingale & Company, 1994).

Finishing Up

You are almost ready to sit back and relax with your beautiful flannel quilt! Follow the steps below to apply binding and a label to your creation.

Binding

Each project in this book calls for binding strips cut 2½" wide across the width of the fabric. The strips are pieced to create one long strip of binding. You will need enough strips to go around the perimeter of your quilt plus an additional 10" to allow for seams and turning the corners.

1. Trim the batting and backing even with the edges of your quilt top.

2. Sew the binding strips together to create one long strip. Place the strips at right angles to each other, right sides together. Draw a diagonal line as shown. Stitch on the line. Trim ¼" away from the seam. Press the seam allowance open.

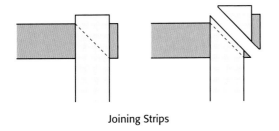

Joining Strips

3. Fold the binding in half lengthwise, wrong sides together. Match the raw edges and press. Trim the selvages from both ends of the binding.

4. Begin sewing your binding to the top of the quilt about 12" away from a corner. Use a walking foot and a ¼" seam allowance. Match all raw edges together and leave an 8" tail of

binding unstitched. Stop sewing when you are ¼" away from the corner. Backstitch to anchor your seam, and remove the quilt from the machine.

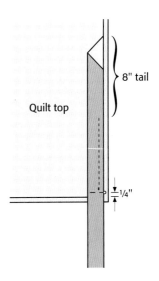

8" tail

Quilt top

¼"

ACCURATE SEAMS WITH A WALKING FOOT

If you normally rely on a ¼" patchwork foot to guide you to an accurate ¼" seam allowance, you may be out of luck once you attach a walking foot to your machine. This attachment is definitely wider than ¼".

You'll either need to mark the seam allowance on the machine bed with tape, or you can try this: Move the needle one or two positions to the right so that more of your quilt can be under the walking foot to feed evenly. It looks like you'll be feeding your quilt through the machine along the ⅝" seam allowance, but by moving the needle position to the right, you can still get a ¼" seam allowance while benefiting from the even-feed feature of the walking foot. If you stick to following the ¼" marking, only ¼" of your quilt edge will go under the walking foot, and the right side of the walking foot will barely touch the fabric.

5. Rotate your quilt a quarter turn so that the next side is ready to stitch. Fold the binding up and away from the quilt. Form a 45° fold, checking to make sure that the raw edges of the binding and the quilt line up with each other. Next, fold the binding back down on itself. Again, all raw edges must be aligned. Stitch the binding in place on this side of the quilt. Repeat the previous steps each time you come to a corner.

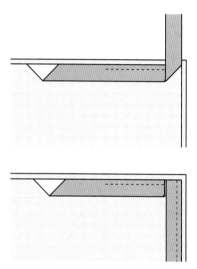

6. On the last side of the quilt, stop stitching about 8" from the edge of the loose tail. Backstitch to secure the seam and remove the quilt from the machine. Lay the end of the binding on top of the beginning tail. Make sure your quilt and binding tails are flat. Make a mark on the ending tail, 2½" longer than the edge of the beginning tail. Check your mark again. (When in a hurry, I've been known to mark and cut the ending tail 2½" shorter. That's frustrating!) Cut across the binding to remove the excess fabric.

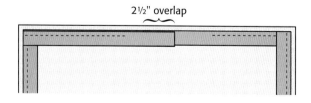

2½" overlap

7. Unfold the ends of the binding. Place the fabric right sides together, forming a right angle. Draw a diagonal line on the wrong side of the fabric as shown. Pin ends together.

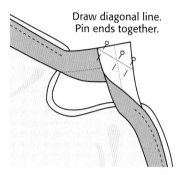

Draw diagonal line.
Pin ends together.

8. Sew on the marked line. Trim ¼" away from the seam and press the seam allowance open. Refold the binding, line up all the raw edges, and finish sewing it in place.

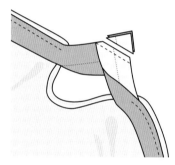

9. Fold the binding to the back of the quilt. The fold should cover the stitching you just completed. Miter the corners as you go. Hand or machine stitch in place. Yes, I often machine stitch bindings on "utility" quilts and have not been struck by lightning yet!

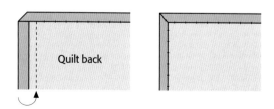

Quilt back

⚇ *Binding by Machine* ⚇

If you want to attach a binding entirely by machine from start to finish, I recommend starting by sewing the binding strips to the back of the quilt first. After it is attached, fold the binding to the front of the quilt to cover the line of stitching. You can use a variety of machine stitches to anchor it in place including a straight stitch, blanket stitch, blind stitch, or other decorative stitch. My current favorite is a zigzag stitch.

I set the stitch length to 3 and the width to 1.5. I move the needle position all the way to the right so that the walking foot is on the fabric as much as possible, and then sew as close to the fold as I can. It makes a wavy sort of stitching line that doesn't attract too much attention to itself.

Label It!

Labeling your quilt is the finishing touch. It is truly amazing how quickly the details are forgotten. One of the saddest things I ever saw was a book full of magnificent quilts. On page after page they were identified merely as "maker unknown." Please take a few moments to ensure that won't happen to your quilts. At least include your name, city and state, finish date, and the name of the quilt. Any other pertinent information should also be included, such as the name of the recipient or your inspiration for creating the quilt. Have a little fun with it! I include an Ogham alphabet picture of my name (Ogham is an ancient Celtic alphabet) and a Nine Patch block on my labels for a truly personal touch.

THE MOON AND THE STARS

Combine a celestial flannel print with two coordinating fabrics and give that special someone the moon and the stars. No need to let on how easy this quilt is to make. One simple block, rotated just so, sends a zigzag pattern chasing across this sweet little quilt. Why not make one for yourself while you're at it?

Materials

All yardages are based on 42"-wide fabrics.

- 1¾ yards of blue print for blocks, borders, and binding
- 1¼ yards of celestial print for blocks
- ¾ yard of gold print for blocks
- 3⅛ yards of backing fabric
- 48" x 66" piece of batting

Cutting

All cutting dimensions include ¼" seam allowances.

From the blue print, cut:
- 12 strips, 3½" x 42"
- 6 binding strips, 2½" x 42"

From the gold print, cut:
- 6 strips, 3½" x 42"

From the celestial print, cut:
- 6 strips, 6½" x 42"; crosscut into 54 rectangles, 3½" x 6½"

Three Patch Block Construction

Before you begin, refer to the instructions for strip piecing and pressing on page 11.

1. Place a 3½"-wide blue strip and a 3½"-wide gold strip right sides together. Sew from selvage to selvage. Press seam allowances open. Repeat until you have six strip sets. Trim the selvage edges.

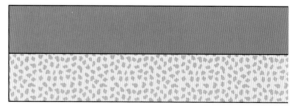

Make 6 strip sets.

2. Crosscut the strip sets into 3½"-wide segments. You will need 54 segments.

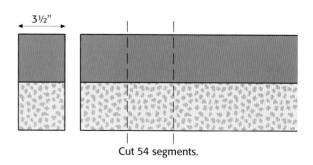

Cut 54 segments.

By Beth Garretson, 2003, Yakima, Washington.
Finished quilt size: 42" x 60" ▪ Finished block size: 6" x 6"

3. Place the segments right sides together with the celestial-print rectangles as shown. Sew seams on the long side of the rectangles. Press the seam allowances open. How easy was that?

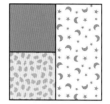

Three Patch Block
Make 54.

Quilt Assembly

See page 12 for instructions on assembling a straight-set quilt.

1. Arrange the blocks according to the diagram below. Make five of row A and four of row B. Pay close attention to the way your blocks are rotated within the rows so that when the rows are assembled you'll have a stair-step design.

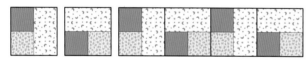

Row A
Make 5.

Row B
Make 4.

2. Sew the rows together. Begin with a row A. Alternate rows A and B, carefully placing each row in the proper direction.

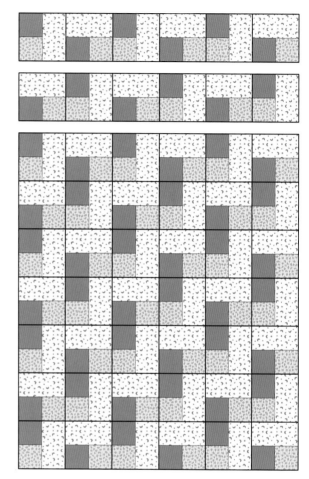

Quilt Assembly

🌙 KEEPING TRACK OF ROWS 🌙

When a quilt plan calls for alternating rows, I like to label them. For this quilt, cut a piece of scrap paper into squares. Label five of them "A" and four of them "B." Attach the labels to the upper left corner of each row with a safety pin. This little extra step will keep your rows in order and turned the proper way.

3. Sew the 3½"-wide blue top and bottom borders to the quilt first, referring to pages 12–13 for instructions on measuring and trimming borders to fit. Then join a pair of 3½"-wide border strips to make a long side border. Repeat for the other side border. Attach the side borders in the same manner as for the top and bottom borders.

Finishing

1. Cut the backing fabric into two equal lengths and sew the pieces together to make a backing with a horizontal seam. Press the seam allowance open. Trim the backing so that it is approximately 6" larger than the quilt top.

2. Layer the quilt top with the backing and batting; baste. Machine quilt as desired. To emphasize the zigzag pattern, I did some channel quilting with my walking foot on the celestial fabric. The border is quilted with free-motion moons and stars.

3. Trim excess backing and batting even with the edges of the quilt top.

4. Use the 2½"-wide blue strips to bind your quilt. Refer to pages 15–17 for basic binding instructions.

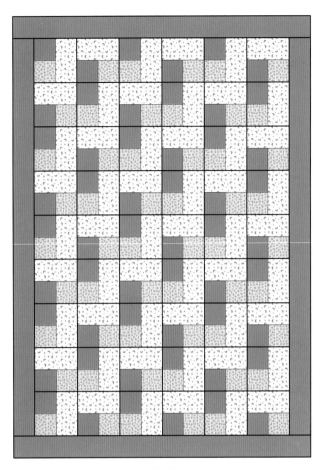

Quilt Plan

COLOR OPTIONS

You can easily change the mood of this quilt by using seasonal prints.

A BIT OF BARGELLO

Brightly colored flannels give this quilt a whimsical personality. With only five fabrics to choose, this design can easily be translated into a more sophisticated palette. Simple strip-piecing construction promises fast results for quilters of every skill level.

Materials

For a successful bargello design, include fabrics ranging from light to dark and with a variety of print textures.

All yardages are based on 42"-wide fabrics.

- 1¼ yard of cat print for strip sets and binding
- ¾ yard of swirly print for strip sets
- ¾ yard of green print for strip sets
- ¾ yard of multicolor print for strip sets
- ¾ yard of lavender print for strip sets
- 3¼ yards of backing fabric
- 51" x 66" piece of batting

Cutting

All cutting dimensions include ¼" seam allowances.

From each of the five quilt fabrics, cut:

- 3 strips, 6½" x 42" (15 strips total). Cut 1 strip of each fabric in half crosswise, for 10 full-width and ten half-width strips.

From the cat print, cut:

- 6 binding strips, 2½" x 42"

Strip-Set Construction

Before you begin, refer to the instructions for strip piecing and pressing on page 11.

1. Arrange the 6½" x 42" strips in the following order: swirly print, green print, cat print, multicolor print, lavender print. Then repeat the order. With right sides together, sew pairs of strips from selvage edge to selvage edge. Press seam allowances open. Sew the pairs of strips together, lining up selvages at one end, until the strip set is completed. Press seam allowances open after each addition.

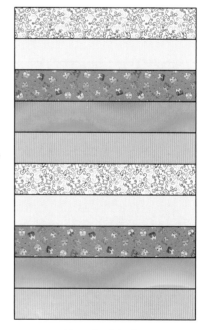

Bargello Strip Set

By Beth Garretson, 2003, Yakima, Washington
Finished quilt size: 45" x 60"

2. Repeat this procedure with the 6½" x 21" strips, making sure the fabrics are arranged in the same order as the long strips. You'll have one full-length and one shorter strip set.

3. Sew the long edges of each strip set together, lining up the selvages on one end of the strip set, to form a tube. Press the seam open and turn the tube right side out.

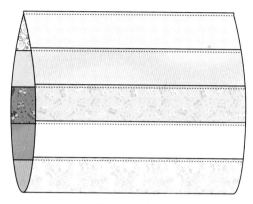

Bargello Tube

Cutting Segments

To make the quilt shown, you will need to cut the tubes into strips that run parallel to the selvages. Then, each strip needs to be cut at one point and opened out into a long, pieced strip. To create the bargello effect, you need to cut each strip at a different point.

If each strip is separated at a seam, each row aligns with the next row precisely at the seam lines. Each segment moves a whole step. The design shown uses a half-step method, which means that every other strip is separated at a seam, and the remaining strips are separated in the center of a segment between two seams. The half-step method means that when the strips are joined back together to form the quilt top, there are no seams to match up. Yeah!

1. Lay a bargello tube on the cutting mat. Gently position the fabric so that all seam lines are parallel with each other. Position the horizontal ruler markings so that they are parallel with the seams. Trim off the selvages at the end of the strip set where all the selvages are aligned.

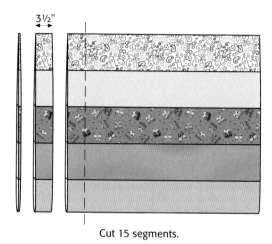

Cut 15 segments.

2. Crosscut the tubes into 3½"-wide segments. After a few cuts, check to make sure markings on your ruler are still parallel with the seams. If not, trim a small amount away to regain a straight edge. Continue cutting until you have 15 segments.

3. Refer to the bargello cutting plan (opposite) to determine where each strip should be cut. Arrows on the chart pointing downward indicate that you will move one half step down the strip before you cut. Arrows pointing upward indicate that you will move one half step up the strip for your next cut.

Beginning with the first strip, cut every other row (the odd-numbered ones) at the seam between neighboring fabrics. Simply cut off the seam with your rotary cutter. Cut the remaining rows (the even-numbered ones) through the exact center of a fabric segment, which should be 3" from a seam. I always check off each segment as I go. It is very easy to make the same cut twice unless you keep track of your progress.

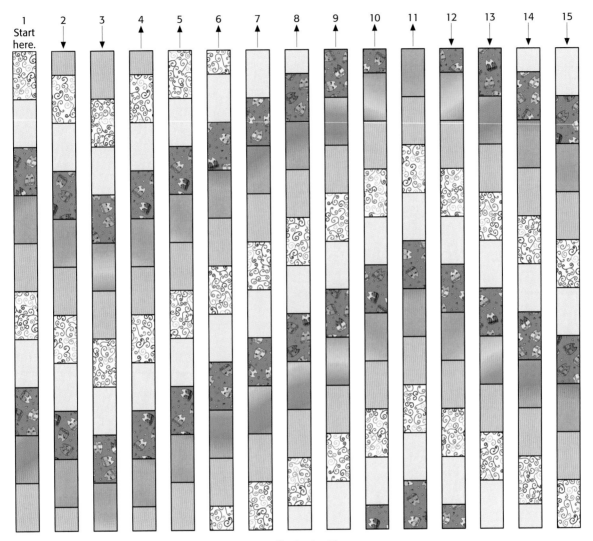

1
Start
here.

2 3 4 5 6 7 8 9 10 11 12 13 14 15

Bargello Cutting Plan

Quilt Assembly

1. Arrange the segments in order according to the cutting plan.

2. Pin a pair of segments right sides together and sew them together along the long edges. Press the seam allowances open.

3. Continue pinning and sewing pairs until all segments are joined together.

Finishing

1. Cut the backing fabric into two equal lengths and sew the pieces together to make a backing with a horizontal seam. Press the seam allowance open. Trim the backing so that it is approximately 6" larger than the quilt top.

2. Layer the quilt top with the backing and batting; baste. Machine quilt as desired. "A Bit of Bargello" was quilted with free-motion waves that gently follow the curved design. Five different variegated cotton threads enhance the joyful spirit of this quilt.

3. Trim excess backing and batting even with the edges of the quilt top.

4. Use the 2½"-wide cat print strips to bind your quilt. Refer to pages 15–17 for basic binding instructions.

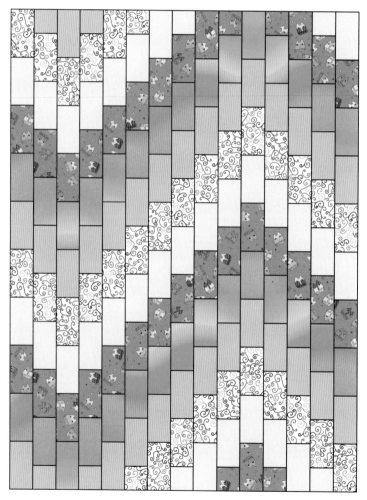

Quilt Plan

SQUARES DANCE!

This dreamy quilt looks complicated yet is very easy to create. Large blocks with simple components fill the design with squares sashaying across the quilt top. The large border contains all the activity and gives you space to show off your quilting skills.

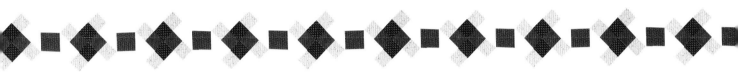

Materials

All yardages are based on 42"-wide fabrics.

- 3¾ yards of floral print for blocks, borders, and binding
- 1⅛ yard of pink print for blocks
- 1 yard of off-white print for blocks
- ½ yard of dark green print for blocks
- 5 yards of backing fabric
- 66" x 78" piece of batting

USING DIRECTIONAL FABRICS

I tend to sort prints into three categories. Allover (or non-directional) prints can be cut and sewn without any special care. Directional prints, such as stripes, require a bit more planning to ensure that the lines are running consistently either horizontally or vertically. If the directional print also has a top and bottom to it, such as an animal or a person, I check my pieces very carefully before I sew them together.

Directional fabrics can add a nice spark to your quilt designs. The extra care is worth the time it takes to assure proper placement.

Cutting

All cutting dimensions include ¼" seam allowances.

From the floral print, cut:

- 5 strips, 3⅞" x 42"; crosscut into 40 squares, 3⅞" x 3⅞". Cut each square once diagonally to yield 80 triangles.
- 8 strips, 3½" x 42"
- 8 strips, 6½" x 42"
- 8 binding strips, 2½" x 42"

From the pink print fabric, cut:

- 4 strips, 4¾" x 42"; crosscut into 30 squares, 4¾" x 4¾"
- 4 strips, 3½" x 42"

From the off-white print, cut:

- 8 strips, 3½" x 42"

From the dark green print, cut:

- 4 strips, 3½" x 42"

By Beth Garretson, 2003, Yakima, Washington; machine quilted by Michaela Hughes
Finished quilt size: 60" x 72" ■ Finished block size: 12" x 12"

Susannah Block Construction

Before you begin, refer to the instructions for strip piecing and pressing on page 11. Throughout the piecing, sew triangles to squares with the square fabric on top to reduce distortion.

1. Center the long edge of a triangle along one edge of a square, right sides together. Sew and press the seam allowance open. Center another triangle on the opposite side of the square. Sew and press the seam allowance open.

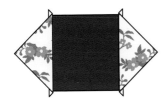

2. Center a triangle on the remaining two sides of the block. Sew and press the seam allowances open. Repeat to make 20 square-in-a-square units.

Square-in-a-Square
Make 20.

3. Place 3½"-wide strips of floral and off-white fabric right sides together. Sew together along the long edge. Press the seam allowance open. Repeat to make a total of four strip sets. Trim

the selvages off of the strip sets and then cross-cut the strip sets into 3½"-wide segments. You will need 40 segments.

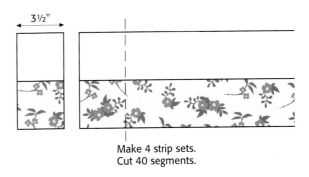

Make 4 strip sets.
Cut 40 segments.

4. Place a segment on the top and bottom of a square-in-a-square unit, right sides together. Make sure your segments are turned the correct direction; refer to the illustration below. Match and pin seams. Stitch; press the seam allowances open. Repeat to make 20 partial blocks.

Note: The next instructions for strip sets are divided into two phases because I used a directional print. If none of your prints are directional, you may construct all of the strip sets identically.

5. Arrange one each of the remaining 3½"-wide strips in the following order: dark green print, off-white print, floral print, and pink print. With right sides together, sew pairs of strips from selvage edge to selvage edge. Press the seam allowances open. Sew the pairs to each other and press. Repeat to make two strip sets.

Crosscut the strip sets into 3½"-wide segments. You will need 20 segments.

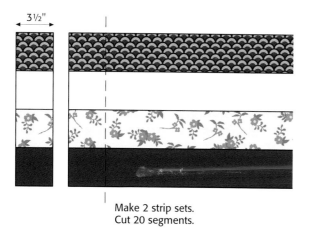

Make 2 strip sets.
Cut 20 segments.

6. Place a segment on the *left* side of a partial block, right sides together. Make sure that the segment is turned the correct direction; refer to the illustration below. Match and pin the seam. Stitch and then press the seam allowance open. Repeat for all 20 partial blocks.

7. Arrange one each of the remaining 3½" strips in the following order: pink print, floral print, off-white print, and dark green print. With right sides together, sew pairs of strips from selvage to selvage. Press the seam allowances open. Sew the pairs of strips together in the specified color order. Press the seam allowances open. Repeat to make two identical strip sets.

Crosscut the strip sets in segments 3½"-wide. You will need 20 segments.

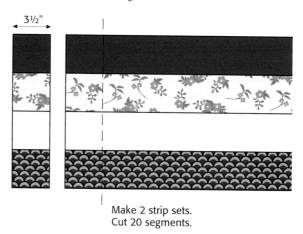

Make 2 strip sets.
Cut 20 segments.

8. Place a segment on the *right* side of a partial block, right sides together. Make sure that the segment is turned the correct direction; refer to the illustration below. Match and pin the seam. Stitch and the press the seam allowance open. Repeat to complete 20 Susannah blocks.

Susannah Block
Make 20.

Quilt Assembly

See page 12 for instructions on assembling a straight-set quilt. In this setting, all blocks are positioned the same way; none are rotated.

1. Arrange the blocks into five rows of four blocks each as shown. Sew the blocks together in horizontal rows.

2. Sew the rows together.

3. Join pairs of 6½"-wide border strips end to end to yield four long border strips. See pages 12–13 for instructions on measuring and applying borders to fit.

Finishing

1. Cut the backing fabric into two equal lengths and sew the pieces together to make a backing with a vertical seam. Press the seam allowance open. Trim the backing so that it is approximately 6" larger than the quilt top.

2. Layer the quilt top with the backing and batting; baste. Machine quilt as desired. "Squares Dance!" was professionally quilted by Michaela Hughes with green variegated thread. The pattern she used, Floral Meandering, was designed by Dave Hudson.

3. Trim excess backing and batting even with the edges of the quilt top.

4. Use the 2½"-wide floral print strips to bind your quilt. Refer to pages 15–17 for basic binding instructions.

Quilt Plan

ZIGZAG

The secret to this quilt's energetic design is block rotation and the use of two different fabrics in the setting triangles. One simple block is all you need to construct this lively pattern. The block is based on a Courthouse Steps arrangement. Because it has only five pieces, I decided to call it the Few-Step block. "Zigzag" is a twin-size quilt that will certainly brighten up any room in your home!

Materials

All yardages are based on 42"-wide fabrics. Because this is a diagonal set, it is best to avoid strong directional prints.

- 2 yards of purple fabric for blocks and setting triangles
- 2 yards of large-scale floral print for blocks and setting triangles
- 1 yard of off-white print for blocks
- ½ yard of red print for blocks
- ¾ yard of small-scale floral print for binding
- 5⅓ yards of backing fabric
- 62" x 87" piece of batting

Cutting

All cutting dimensions include ¼" seam allowance.

From the off-white print, cut:
- 8 strips, 3½" x 42"

From the red fabric, cut:
- 4 strips, 3½" x 42"

From the purple fabric, cut:
- 4 strips, 9½" x 42"; crosscut into 39 rectangles, 9½" x 3½"
- 2 squares, 14¼" x 14¼"; cut each square twice diagonally to yield 8 triangles
- 2 squares, 7½" x 7½"; cut each square once diagonally to yield four triangles (set one aside; you need only three)

From the large-scale floral print, cut:
- 4 strips, 9½" x 42"; crosscut into 39 rectangles, 9½" x 3½"
- 2 squares, 14¼" x 14¼"; cut each square twice diagonally to yield 8 triangles
- 1 square, 7½" x 7½"; cut the square once diagonally to yield 2 triangles (set one aside; you need only one)

From the small-scale floral print, cut:
- 8 binding strips, 2½" x 42"

By Beth Garretson, 2003, Yakima, Washington
Finished quilt size: 55½" x 81" ■ Finished block size: 9" x 9"

Few-Step Block Construction

Before you begin, refer to the instructions for strip piecing and pressing on page 11.

1. Place 3½"-wide strips of off-white and red fabric right sides together. Sew from selvage to selvage. Press the seam allowances open. Repeat until you have four pairs of strips. Place the remaining off-white strips right sides together with the red fabric of your strip pairs. Sew from selvage to selvage. Press the seam allowances open. Repeat until you have four strip sets. Crosscut the strip sets into segments 3½" wide. You will need 39 segments.

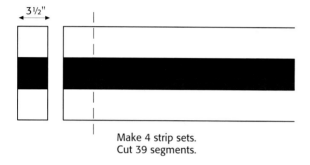

3½"

Make 4 strip sets.
Cut 39 segments.

2. Place the segments right sides together with the purple rectangles. Stitch on the long side of the rectangle. Press the seam allowances open.

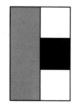

3. Place the floral print rectangles on the opposite sides of the segments, right sides together, referring to the illustration below for proper placement. Sew seams on the long side of the rectangles. Press the seam allowances open.

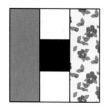

Few-Step Block
Make 39.

Quilt Assembly

See page 12 for instructions on assembling a diagonal set.

1. Lay the finished blocks and the setting-triangle fabrics in separate stacks.

2. Referring to the quilt assembly diagram, sew the blocks and setting triangles into rows. Pay close attention to the way your blocks are rotated within the rows; otherwise, your finished quilt won't have the desired zigzag effect. Be sure to use setting triangles of the correct fabrics at the beginning and end of each row.

3. Sew the rows together.

EASY-ASSEMBLY DIAGONAL SETS

If this is the first time you have constructed a diagonal-set quilt, the following ideas will make the process easier for you.

- Make a copy of your quilt assembly plan and keep it close to your sewing machine. Check off the rows as you sew them together to avoid repeating a row.

- I like to place my triangles and blocks directly on the plan to ensure that they are turned the correct way before sewing them together. As soon as you place two pieces together, put a pin on the side you intend to sew. It's easy to get them turned around.

- Match the right-angle corner of the side setting triangles with the corner of the block you'll be sewing it to. Remember, the triangles are cut oversized, so you'll have extra long "dog ears" at the outer edge of the quilt top.

4. Square up the quilt top by trimming excess fabric from the setting triangles. Note that on the quilt shown, I left 2" extra beyond the edges of the blocks on each side of the quilt. This gives the appearance that the quilt has a border on each side.

Finishing

1. Cut the backing fabric into two equal lengths and sew the pieces together to make a backing with a vertical seam. Press the seam allowance open. Trim the backing so that it is approximately 6" larger than the quilt top.

2. Layer the quilt top with the batting and the backing; baste. Machine quilt as desired. "Zigzag" is lightly quilted with variegated thread, emphasizing the eye-catching geometric pattern created by the block rotations. Free-motion quilting in the red squares emphasizes their role as the accent fabric in this project.

3. Trim excess backing and batting even with the edges of the quilt top.

4. Use the 2½"-wide small-scale floral print strips to bind your quilt. Refer to pages 15–17 for basic binding instructions.

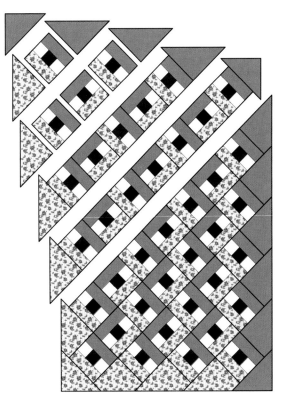

Quilt Assembly

ꙮ COLOR OPTION ꙮ

Done up in bright prints, "Zigzag" will be a hit with the younger (or young-at-heart) crowd!

October Afternoon

Autumn is an amazing season in the Yakima Valley of Washington State. While the days remain warm and sunny, the nights are suddenly cool and crisp. There is a great rush to harvest grapes and apples before the snow flies. Flowers and foliage take on a deep glow before frost sends the garden off to sleep for the winter. It is my favorite time of year! "October Afternoon" captures this feeling with its rich colors. No-fuss Four Patch and Nine Patch blocks make for quick construction of this full-size quilt.

Materials

All yardages are based on 42"-wide fabrics.

- 3¼ yards of large-scale floral print for blocks and borders
- 2⅛ yards of gold fabric for blocks and binding
- 1¾ yards of green print fabric for blocks
- 1½ yards of small-scale floral print for blocks and borders
- 1¼ yards of pink print for blocks
- 8 yards of backing fabric
- 85" x 103" piece of batting

Cutting

All cutting dimensions include ¼" seam allowances.

From the gold fabric, cut:
- 9 strips, 5" x 42"
- 10 binding strips, 2½" x 42"

From the large-scale floral print, cut:
- 9 strips, 5" x 42"
- 10 strips, 6½" x 42"

From the pink print, cut:
- 11 strips, 3½" x 42"

From the green print, cut:
- 15 strips, 3½" x 42"

From the small-scale floral print, cut:
- 7 strips, 3½" x 42"
- 9 strips, 2½" x 42"

By Beth Garretson, 2003, Yakima, Washington; machine quilted by Michaela Hughes
Finished quilt size: 79" x 97" ■ Finished block size: 9" x 9"

Block Construction

Before you begin, refer to the instructions for strip piecing and pressing on page 11.

Four Patch Blocks

1. Place 5"-wide strips of gold fabric and large-scale floral print in pairs, right sides together. Sew them together along one long edge. Press the seam allowances open. Repeat to make a total of nine strip sets. Crosscut the strip sets into segments 5" wide. You will need 62 segments.

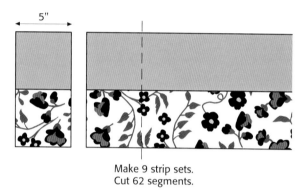

Make 9 strip sets.
Cut 62 segments.

2. Place the segments in pairs, right sides together, with opposite fabrics touching each other. Match and pin seams. Stitch on the long side and press the seam allowances open. You will have 31 Four Patch blocks.

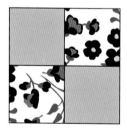

Four Patch Block
Make 31.

Nine Patch Blocks

1. Place 3½"-wide strips of pink and green prints right sides together. Sew them together along one long edge. Press the seam allowances open. Repeat to make a total of seven pairs of strips. Then sew 3½"-wide strips of small-scale floral print, right sides together, to the green fabric of the strip pairs. Press the seam allowances open. Repeat for all seven strip sets.

Crosscut the strip sets into 3½"-wide segments. You will need 64 segments.

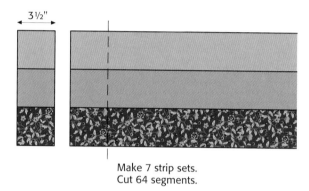

Make 7 strip sets.
Cut 64 segments.

2. In the same manner as for the strip sets from step 1, make four strip sets using the 3½"-wide strips of green and pink fabric. The pink fabric should be in the center, with a green strip on either side. Make four of these strip sets and press the seam allowances open.

Crosscut the strip sets into 3½"-wide segments. You will need 32 segments.

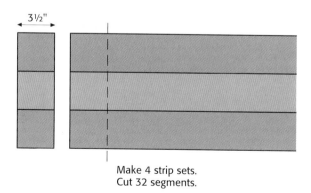

Make 4 strip sets.
Cut 32 segments.

3. Arrange the segments in three stacks so that the pink squares form a diagonal through the block. Sew the segments right sides together, matching and pinning seams. Press the seam allowances open. You will have 32 Nine Patch blocks.

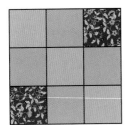

Nine Patch Block
Make 32.

Quilt Assembly

Time to put it all together! See page 12 for instructions on assembling a straight-set quilt.

1. Arrange the blocks into A and B rows, following the diagram below. You will need five of row A and four of row B. Press the seam allowances open.

Row A
Make 5.

Row B
Make 4.

2. Sew the rows together, beginning with a row A on top and alternating rows A and B.

3. Piece the small-scale floral 2½"-wide inner border strips and the 6½"-wide outer border strips together to obtain the required length. See pages 12–13 for instructions on measuring and applying borders. On this quilt, the side borders are attached first, followed by the top and bottom borders.

Quilt Plan

Finishing

1. Cut the backing fabric into three equal lengths and sew the pieces together to make a backing with two horizontal seams. Press the seam allowance open. Trim the backing so that it is approximately 6" larger than the quilt top.

2. Layer the quilt top with the backing and batting; baste. Machine quilt as desired. Michaela Hughes captured the mood of this quilt using an autumn-toned variegated thread and a quilting pattern called Morning Oak by Kimberly Darwin. Swirls and leaves drift across the quilt top, reminding one of a breezy October afternoon.

3. Trim excess backing and batting even with the edges of the quilt top.

4. Use the 2½"-wide gold strips to bind your quilt. Refer to pages 15–17 for basic binding instructions.

TRELLIS

The design for "Trellis" grew from a deep admiration for Celtic knot work and a desire to achieve that look with easy piecing methods. Two contrasting fabrics and two basic blocks are all it takes to form the interlocking pattern of this twin-size quilt. I think you will be pleasantly surprised by the small amount of time required to create this seemingly intricate project.

Materials

All yardages are based on 42"-wide fabrics. Because this is a diagonal set, it is best to avoid strong directional prints.

- 4 yards of floral print for blocks, setting triangles, and binding
- 2 yards of gold fabric for blocks
- 5¼ yards of backing fabric
- 57" x 83" piece of batting

Cutting

All cutting dimensions include ¼" seam allowances.

From the gold fabric, cut:
- 13 strips, 2½" x 42"; crosscut into 30 rectangles, 2½" x 5½" and 30 rectangles, 2½" x 9½"
- 7 strips 3⅛" x 42"; crosscut into 76 squares, 3⅛" x 3⅛"

From the floral print, cut:
- 3 strips, 5½" x 42"; crosscut into 15 squares, 5½" x 5½"
- 6 strips, 9½" x 42"; crosscut into 24 squares, 9½" x 9½"
- 2 strips 14¼" x 42"; crosscut into 4 squares, 14¼" x 14¼". Cut each square twice diagonally to yield 16 triangles.

- 2 squares, 7½" x 7½". Cut each square once diagonally to yield 4 triangles.
- 8 binding strips, 2½" x 42"

Block Construction

Before you begin, refer to the instructions for chain-piecing on page 10 and pressing on page 11.

Framed Square Block

I like to strip piece whenever possible; however, this block makes better use of your fabric when it is precut into rectangles.

1. Place a 5½"-long gold rectangle on a 5½" floral print square, right sides together. Sew and press the seam allowance open. Place another gold rectangle on the opposite side of the square, right sides together. Sew and press. Repeat until you have 15 partial blocks.

Make 15.

By Beth Garretson, 2003, Yakima, Washington
Finished quilt size: 51½" x 77" ■ Finished block sizes: 9" x 9"

2. Sew the 9½"-long gold rectangles to the remaining sides of the floral squares, right sides together. Press the seam allowances open. Repeat to complete all 15 blocks.

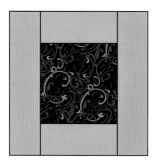

Framed Square Block
Make 15.

Snowball Block

These blocks are constructed in three groups according to how many corner squares they require.

1. Place a gold square on the corner of a 9½" floral print square, right sides together. Mark a line from corner to corner on the back of the gold square and then sew on the line. Trim the excess fabric ¼" away from the seam and press open.

Stitch.   Trim.

Press open.

✿ PERFECT FOLDED CORNERS ✿

Instead of sewing directly on the line you marked from corner to corner on the small squares, sew one needle width to the outside of the line (toward the part you will trim off). This gives you just the little bit of insurance you need to have the finished corners lie flat and square.

2. Continue to add gold squares to the corners of floral squares until you have 4 blocks with two gold corners, 12 blocks with three gold corners, and 8 blocks with four gold corners, for a total of 24 blocks.

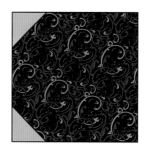 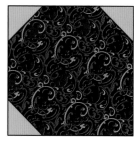

Make 4.   Make 12.

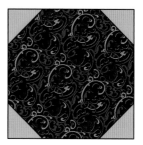

Make 8.

Quilt Assembly

See page 12 for instructions on assembling a diagonal-set quilt.

1. Separate the three types of Snowball blocks, the Framed Square blocks, and the two types of setting triangles into six separate stacks.

2. Referring to the quilt assembly diagram, arrange the blocks and setting triangles into rows. Pay close attention to the way your blocks are rotated within the rows. When you are satisfied that all blocks are arranged correctly, sew them together in rows. Press the seam allowances open.

3. Sew the rows together and press. Square up quilt top.

Finishing

1. Cut the backing fabric into two equal lengths and sew the pieces together to make a backing with a vertical seam. Press the seam allowances open. Trim the backing so that it is approximately 6" larger than the quilt top.

2. Layer the quilt top with the batting and the backing; baste. Machine quilt as desired. In the project shown, free-motion spirals and echo quilting enhance the Celtic appearance of this project.

3. Trim the excess backing and batting even with the edges of the quilt top.

4. Use the 2½"-wide floral print strips to bind your quilt. Refer to pages 15–17 for basic binding instructions.

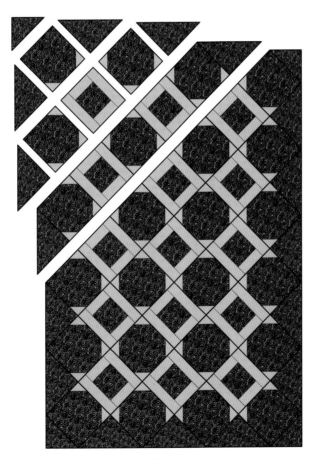

Quilt Assembly

WINDJAMMER

Inspired by the bold colors of nautical signal flags, this queen-size quilt will keep you warm on a blustery night. Two simple blocks set on point result in a dynamic pattern of stars and give the impression of a pieced border. "Windjammer" provides you with smooth sailing through a substantial quilting project.

Materials

All yardages are based on 42"-wide fabrics. Because this quilt is set diagonally, it is best to avoid strong directional prints.

- 4 yards of navy blue fabric for blocks, setting triangles, and binding
- 2¾ yards of golden yellow fabric for blocks
- 2¼ yards of off-white fabric for blocks
- 1½ yards of periwinkle fabric for blocks
- 1⅓ yards of red fabric for blocks
- 8¾ yards of backing fabric
- 91" x 108" piece of batting

Cutting

All cutting dimensions include ¼" seam allowances.

From the golden yellow fabric, cut:
- 8 strips, 6⅞" x 42"; crosscut into 40 squares, 6⅞" x 6⅞". Cut each square once diagonally to yield 80 triangles.
- 6 strips, 5⅛" x 42"; crosscut into 40 squares, 5⅛" x 5⅛". Cut each square once diagonally to yield 80 triangles.

From the periwinkle fabric, cut:
- 5 strips, 9" x 42"; crosscut into 20 squares, 9" x 9"

From the navy blue fabric, cut:
- 3 strips, 5⅛" x 42"; crosscut into 20 squares, 5⅛" x 5⅛". Cut each square once diagonally to yield 40 triangles.
- 3 strips, 6⅞" x 42"; crosscut into 11 squares, 6⅞" x 6⅞". Cut each square once diagonally to yield 22 triangles.
- 3 strips, 18½" x 42"; crosscut into 5 squares, 18½" x 18½". Cut each square twice diagonally to yield 20 side-setting triangles. You will only use 18. Use the leftover fabric to cut 2 squares, 9¾" x 9¾". Cut each square once diagonally to yield 4 corner-setting triangles.
- 11 binding strips, 2½" x 42"

From the red fabric, cut:
- 6 strips, 6½" x 42"; crosscut into 30 squares, 6½" x 6½"

From the off-white fabric, cut:
- 10 strips, 6⅞" x 42"; crosscut into 49 squares, 6⅞" x 6⅞". Cut each square once diagonally to yield 98 triangles.

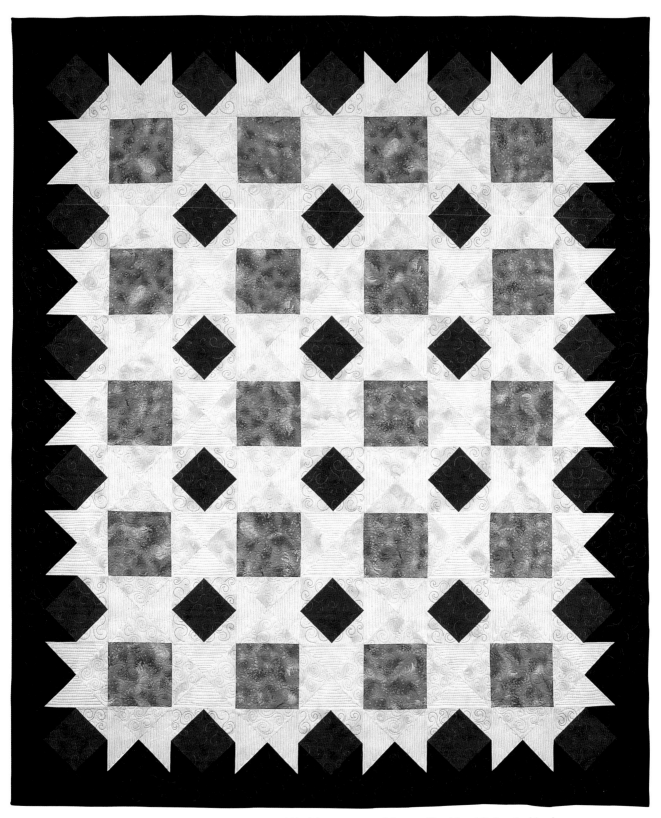

By Beth Garretson, 2003, Yakima, Washington; machine quilted by Michaela Hughes
Finished quilt size: 85" x 102" ■ Finished block size: 12" x 12"

Block Construction

Before you begin, refer to the instructions for chain-piecing on page 10 and pressing on page 11.

With these blocks, always place the large triangles underneath and the squares or small triangles on top for sewing. Then as you sew, the bias edges will be next to the feed dogs and the straight-grain edges will be under the presser foot. This way, the top fabric won't creep ahead of the bottom fabric and distort your blocks.

Square-in-a-Square Block

1. Center a 6⅞" yellow triangle on one edge of a periwinkle square, right sides together. Sew and press the seam allowances open. Center another triangle on the opposite side of the square. Sew and press as before.

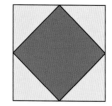

2. Center a 6⅞" yellow triangle on the remaining two sides of the block. Sew and press the seam allowances open. Repeat to make 20 blocks.

Square-in-a-Square Block
Make 20.

Hourglass Block

This block is also known as Economy Patch or the Thrift block. Whatever name you like to use, for this quilt, the blocks are constructed in three different colorations. Pay close attention to the diagrams, and your fabrics will be in the correct position.

1. Center the 5⅛" yellow and navy triangles and sew them to the red squares as you did for the Square-in-a-Square blocks. Refer to the illustration for color placement and quantities. Label the units A, B, and C.

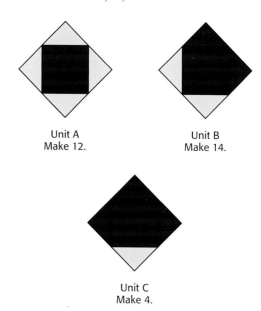

Unit A
Make 12.

Unit B
Make 14.

Unit C
Make 4.

2. Complete the blocks by centering and sewing the 6⅞" off-white and navy triangles to the units you made in the previous step. Refer to the illustration for color placement.

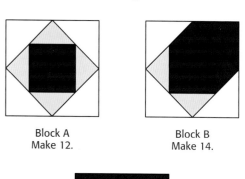

Block A
Make 12.

Block B
Make 14.

Block C
Make 4.

Quilt Assembly

See page 12 for instructions on assembling a diagonal set.

1. Lay the finished blocks and the setting triangles in separate stacks according to color placement.

2. Referring to the quilt assembly diagram, arrange the blocks and setting triangles into rows. Take care to place your Hourglass blocks exactly as they appear in the diagram. Sew the blocks together in rows. Press the seam allowances open.

3. Sew the rows together and press the quilt top.

4. Square up the quilt top by trimming excess fabric from the setting triangles.

Finishing

1. Cut the backing fabric into three equal lengths and sew the pieces together to make a backing with two horizontal seams. Press the seam allowance open. Trim the backing so that it is approximately 6" larger than the quilt top.

2. Layer the quilt top with the batting and backing; baste. Machine quilt as desired. Michaela Hughes quilted "Windjammer" using free-motion stitching in looping rows to emphasize the star points. Spiral patterns stitched in variegated thread complete the look of a cozy quilt designed to deflect cold winds.

3. Trim the excess backing and batting even with the edges of the quilt top.

4. Use the 2½"-wide navy blue strips to bind your quilt. See pages 15–17 for basic binding instructions.

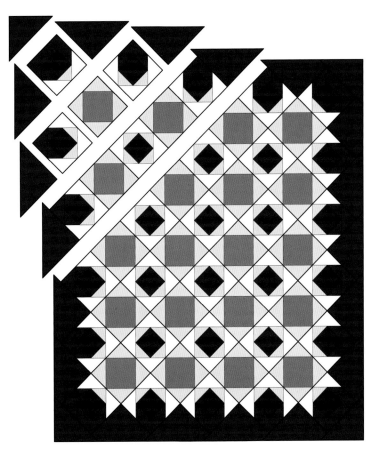

Quilt Assembly

STARGAZER

While designing this quilt I was flooded with memories of a Thanksgiving spent in Tucson, Arizona. My sister-in-law, Eve, and I traced our hands on brown paper bags and then colored our "turkeys" with crayons. We did our after-Thanksgiving shopping in Nogales, Mexico. One evening we drove to the top of a peak outside Tucson where we looked at the city below and the stars above. I fell in love with Southwest-style art and every shade of turquoise. A few simple alterations of an octagon block and jewel-tone colors capture the spirit of my Arizona adventure.

Materials
All yardages are based on 42"-wide fabrics.

- 1¾ yards of black print for blocks, setting triangles, and binding
- 1⅜ yards of red print for blocks
- ¾ yard of gold print for blocks
- ¾ yard of turquoise print for blocks
- ⅓ yard of periwinkle print for blocks
- 3⅜ yards of backing fabric
- 57" x 57" piece of batting

Cutting
All cutting dimensions include ¼" seam allowances.

From the gold print, cut:
- 5 strips, 3½" x 42"; crosscut into 48 squares, 3½" x 3½"

From the red print, cut:
- 4 strips, 9½" x 42"; crosscut into 16 squares, 9½" x 9½"

From the black print, cut:
- 2 strips, 3½" x 42"; crosscut into 16 squares, 3½" x 3½"
- 2 strips, 14½" x 42"; crosscut into 3 squares, 14½" x 14½". Cut each square twice diagonally to yield 12 side-setting triangles. Use the leftover fabric to cut 2 squares, 7½" x 7½". Cut each square once diagonally to yield 4 corner-setting triangles.
- 6 binding strips, 2½" x 42"

From the turquoise print, cut:
- 2 strips, 9½" x 42"; crosscut into 5 squares, 9½" x 9½"

From the periwinkle print, cut:
- 1 strip, 9½" x 42"; crosscut into 4 squares, 9½" x 9½"

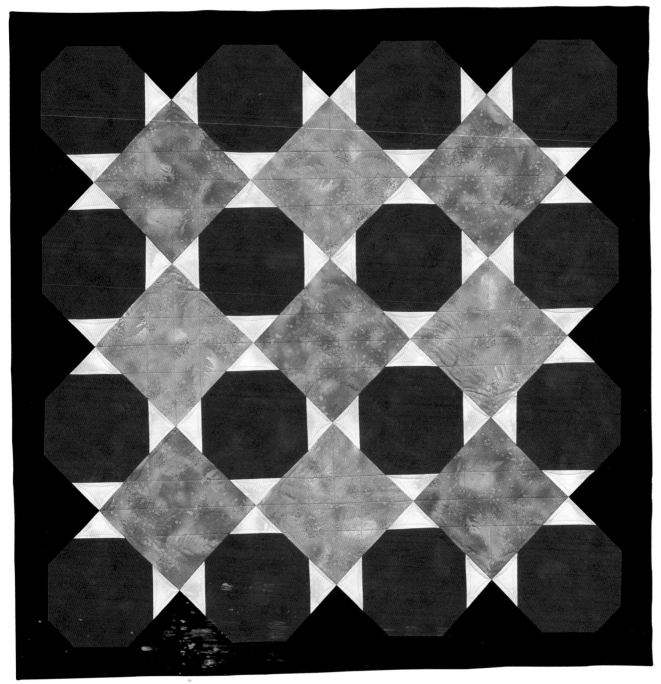

By Beth Garretson, 2003, Yakima, Washington
Finished quilt size: 51" x 51" ■ Finished block size: 9" x 9"

Block Construction

Before you begin, refer to the instructions for chain-piecing on page 10 and pressing on page 11.

The Octagon blocks are constructed in three different colorations. Pay close attention to the diagrams beginning on page 50, and your fabrics will be in the correct position.

1. Place a 3½" gold square right sides together with the corner of a 9½" red square. Mark a line from corner to corner on the back of the gold square, referring to the diagram below. Stitch on the line, and then trim the excess fabric ¼" away from the stitching line. Press the seam allowance open.

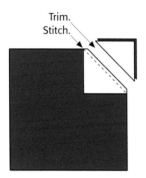

2. Continue to add 3½" gold squares and 3½" black squares to the corners of the red squares until you have a total of 16 Octagon blocks. Refer to the diagram below for color placement. Yes, that's all there is to it!

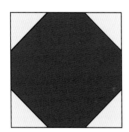

Make 4.

Make 8.

Make 4.

Quilt Assembly

See page 12 for instructions on assembling a diagonal-set quilt.

1. Lay out the finished blocks, plain squares, and setting triangles as shown in the quilt assembly diagram below. Take care to place your Octagon blocks exactly as they appear in the diagram.

Quilt Assembly

2. Referring to the diagram, sew the blocks, plain squares, and setting triangles into rows.

3. Sew the rows together. Press the seams open.

4. Square up the quilt top by trimming excess fabric from the setting triangles.

Finishing

1. Cut the backing fabric into two equal lengths and sew the pieces together to make a backing with a vertical seam. (Or, see the tip box at right.) Press the seam allowance open. Trim the backing so that it is approximately 6" larger than the quilt top.

2. Layer the quilt top with the backing and batting; baste. Machine quilt as desired. "Stargazer" was quilted with free-motion stitching in the Octagon blocks. Straight-line quilting fills the plain squares and border area.

3. Trim the excess backing and batting even with the edges of the quilt top.

4. Use the 2½"-wide black strips to bind your quilt. See pages 15–17 for basic binding instructions.

PIECED BACKING

With "Stargazer" I had lots of the turquoise and periwinkle fabrics left over, but not enough of either one to piece the quilt back. So, I decided to treat the back as one big block. I cut enough 18½" squares to make a large Nine Patch block and then paid close attention to centering the layers as I basted the quilt. Why not try something similar with your flannel leftovers rather than buying extra yardage for a large backing?

Note: This technique works best if you don't have too many seams on the quilt back, and if they don't line up with seams on the quilt top.

COLOR OPTION

With a lovely pansy print featured around the edge of this quilt, "Stargazer" goes from Southwest to English garden.

NINE PATCH MOSAIC

The Nine Patch block offers endless opportunities for design alternatives. In this quilt, three different color-placement options are used, and then corner triangles are added to each Nine Patch, giving the illusion of a diagonal pattern. A checkerboard pieced border surrounds the blocks. Softly colored prints lend a vintage look to this generous throw-size or double-bed size project.

Materials

All yardages are based on 42"-wide fabrics.

- 3 yards of yellow floral print for blocks
- 3 yards of green floral print for blocks, borders, and binding
- 2¼ yards of pink print for blocks and borders
- 7½ yards of backing fabric
- 83" x 83" piece of batting

Cutting

All cutting dimensions include ¼" seam allowances.

From the pink print, cut:
- 9 strips, 3½" x 42"
- 9 strips, 3⅝" x 42"

From the yellow floral print, cut:
- 6 strips, 3½" x 42"
- 10 strips, 7⅛" x 42"; crosscut into 50 squares, 7⅛" x 7⅛". Cut each square once diagonally to yield 100 triangles.

From the green floral print, cut:
- 6 strips, 3½" x 42"
- 4 strips, 3½" x 42"; crosscut into 16 rectangles, 3½" x 9½"

- 9 strips, 3⅝" x 42"
- 9 binding strips, 2½" x 42"

Block Construction

Before you begin, refer to the instructions for strip piecing and pressing on page 11.

Nine Patch Blocks

1. Place a 3½" pink strip right sides together with a 3½" yellow strip. Sew the strips together and press the seam allowance open. Stitch another 3½" pink strip to the other long side of the yellow strip. Press the seam allowance open. Crosscut the strip set into segments 3½" wide. You will need 10 segments.

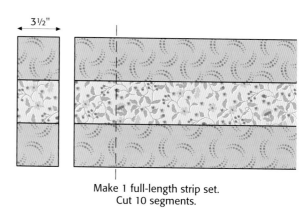

Make 1 full-length strip set.
Cut 10 segments.

By Beth Garretson, 2003, Yakima, Washington
Finished quilt size: 76¾" x 76¾" ■ Finished block size: 12¾" x 12¾"

2. Crosscut one 3½" yellow strip and one 3½" pink strip in half. Place one pink and yellow half-length strip right sides together and sew along the long edge. Press the seam allowance open. Sew the remaining yellow half-length strip, right sides together to the other long edge of the pink half-length strip. Press the seam allowance open. You do not need the remaining half-length strip of pink fabric for this project.

Crosscut the strip set into segments 3½" wide. You will need 5 segments.

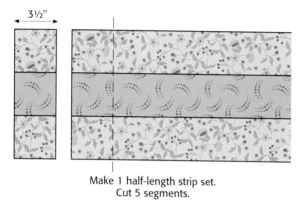

Make 1 half-length strip set.
Cut 5 segments.

3. Arrange the segments as shown below to form Nine Patch blocks. With seams matched, pin and sew the segments together. Press the seam allowances open. You will have five Nine Patch blocks.

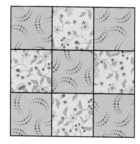

Nine Patch Block
Make 5.

Nine Patch Variation Blocks

1. Cut one 3½" strip each of yellow, green, and pink prints in half crosswise.

2. Place a 3½" pink and 3½" green strip right sides together. Sew the strips together and press the seam allowance open. Repeat to create two full-length strip sets. Pair a 3½" pink and 3½" green half-length strip to create one half-length strip set.

3. Place a 3½" yellow strip right sides together with the green fabric of each strip pair made in step 2. Sew the strips together to complete one half-length and two full-length strip sets. Press the seam allowances open. (Save the remaining half-length strip of pink fabric for step 5. You do not need the remaining half-length strips of green and yellow for this project.)

Crosscut the strip sets into 3½"-wide segments. You will need 24 segments.

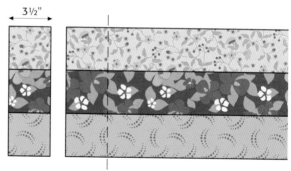

Make 2 full-length strip sets and 1 half-length strip set.
Cut 24 segments.

4. In the same manner as for the yellow, green, and pink strip sets, sew a 3½" pink strip to a 3½" green strip, right sides together. Press the seam allowance open. Then sew another 3½" green strip to the opposite side of the sewn pink strip.

Cut one 3½" green strip in half crosswise and pair these strips with the remaining half-length pink strips from step 2 to make a half-length strip set. Press all seam allowances open. Crosscut the strip sets into 3½"-wide segments. You will need 12 segments.

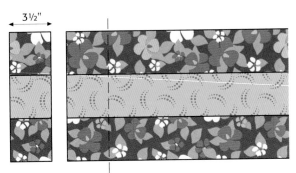

Make 1 full-length strip set and 1 half-length strip set.
Cut 12 segments.

5. Arrange the segments as shown in the diagram below. With seams matched, pin and sew the segments together to complete 12 Nine Patch Variation blocks. Press the seam allowances open.

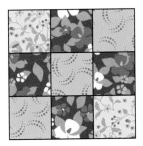

Nine Patch Variation Block
Make 12.

Few-Step Block

1. Place 3½"-wide pink and yellow strips right sides together. Sew the strips together and press the seam allowance open. Sew another 3½"-wide pink strip to the other long edge of the yellow strip and press the seam allowance open. Crosscut the strip set into segments 3½" wide. You will need eight segments.

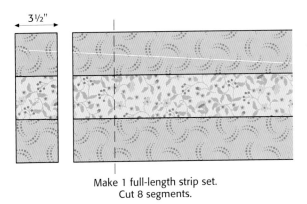

Make 1 full-length strip set.
Cut 8 segments.

2. Sew a 3½" x 9½" green rectangle to opposite sides of the segments from step 1. Press the seam allowances open. You will have eight Few-Step blocks.

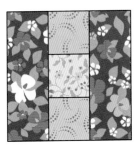

Few-Step Block
Make 8.

Setting Blocks on Point

All of the blocks for this quilt are turned on point by stitching triangles to each side of the blocks. You will essentially be making a square-in-a-square for each block. Follow the directions on page 56, and your blocks will be finished almost before you know it.

1. Center a yellow triangle on one edge of a Nine Patch block, right sides together. Sew and press the seam allowances open. Center another triangle on the opposite side of the block. Sew and press as before.

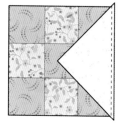

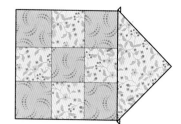

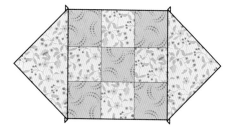

2. Center a yellow triangle on the remaining two sides of the block. Sew and press the seam allowances open. Repeat until all your blocks are on point.

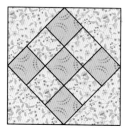

Make 5.

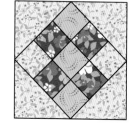

Make 12.

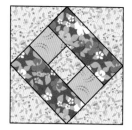

Make 8.

Quilt Assembly

See page 12 for instructions on assembling a straight-set quilt.

1. Arrange the blocks according to the quilt assembly diagram below. Pay close attention to the rotation of the blocks and the placement of the blocks within the rows.

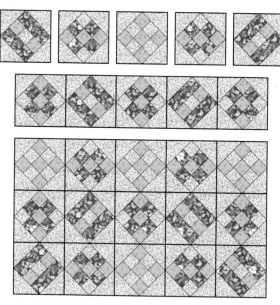

Quilt Assembly

2. Sew the blocks into rows. Press the seam allowances open. Sew the rows together and press as before.

3. Stitch 3⅝"-wide strips of green and pink print right sides together. Press the seam allowances open. Repeat to make a total of nine strip sets. Crosscut the strip sets into segments 3⅝" wide. You will need 88 segments.

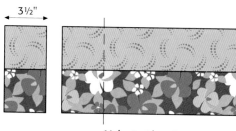

3½"

Make 9 strip sets.
Cut 88 segments.

4. Sew the segments together, right sides facing and seams matching, *using a scant ¼" seam allowance*. Opposite fabrics should be touching one another. Press the seam allowances open. Repeat until you have joined 20 segments each for the side borders and 24 segments each for the top and bottom borders.

5. Sew the side borders to the quilt first, matching the ends of the border to the top and bottom edges of the quilt. Also match the center of the border and quilt; ease as necessary to fit. Press the seam allowances open. Attach the top and bottom borders in the same fashion. Take care when sewing borders to the quilt top to avoid cutting off the points of your blocks.

Side Borders
Make 2.

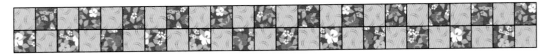

Top and Bottom Borders
Make 2.

Quilt Plan

Finishing

1. Cut the backing fabric into three equal lengths and sew the pieces together to make a backing with two vertical seams. Press the seam allowance open. Trim the backing so that it is approximately 6" larger than the quilt top.

2. Layer the quilt top with the backing and batting; baste. Machine quilt as desired. Beth quilted "Nine Patch Mosaic" with matching cotton threads and free-motion stitching.

3. Trim excess backing and batting even with the edges of the quilt top.

4. Use the 2½"-wide green strips to bind your quilt. Refer to pages 15–17 for basic binding instructions.

COLOR OPTION

Bold colors and lots of contrast give "Nine Patch Mosaic" a completely different look.

DAWN'S STAR

I happen to be a big fan of medallion-style quilts. My idea for this design was to create three stars, each bigger than the next, each different from its neighbor. The original plan called for many half-square triangles, and it looked great on paper. At some point I noticed a fatal flaw: intersections with eight fabrics colliding! As I set about simplifying the construction process, the Half-Off block was created. "Dawn's Star" will make a terrific addition to your home as a wall hanging or favorite lap warmer.

Materials

All yardages are based on 42"- wide fabrics.

- 2 yards of medium-scale floral print for blocks and borders
- 1½ yards of light gold print for blocks
- 1 yard of green print for blocks and binding
- ¾ yard of dark floral print for blocks
- ⅜ yard of deep rust print for blocks
- ¼ yard of brown print for blocks
- ¼ yard of deep gold print for blocks
- 4 yards of backing fabric
- 60" x 60" piece of batting

Cutting

All cutting dimensions include ¼" seam allowances.

From the brown print, cut:
- 1 strip, 3⅞" x 42"; crosscut into 2 squares, 3⅞" x 3⅞". Use the leftover fabric to cut 1 square, 3½" x 3½".

From the deep gold print, cut:
- 1 strip, 3⅞" x 42"; crosscut into 2 squares, 3⅞" x 3⅞". Use the leftover fabric to cut 4 squares, 3½" x 3½".

From the deep rust print, cut:
- 1 strip, 10¼" x 42"; crosscut into 1 square, 10¼" x 10¼". Use the leftover fabric to cut 2 squares, 9⅞" x 9⅞".

From the medium-scale floral print, cut:
- 1 strip, 10¼" x 42"; crosscut into 1 square, 10¼" x 10¼". Set the leftover fabric aside. You may need it for the Half-Off blocks.
- 1 strip, 9½" x 42"; crosscut into 4 squares, 9½" x 9½". Use the leftover fabric from the Star Points blocks (10¼" squares above) if needed.
- 1 strip, 7½" x 42"; crosscut into 4 squares, 7½" x 7½"
- 6 strips, 4½" x 42"

From the green print, cut:
- 1 strip, 7½" x 42"; crosscut into 4 squares, 7½" x 7½"
- 6 binding strips, 2½" x 42"

From the light gold print, cut:
- 2 strips, 9½" x 42"; crosscut into 8 squares, 9½" x 9½"
- 2 strips, 9⅞" x 42"; crosscut into 4 squares, 9⅞" x 9⅞"

From the dark floral print, cut:
- 2 strips, 9⅞" x 42"; crosscut into 4 squares, 9⅞" x 9⅞"

By Beth Garretson, 2003, Yakima, Washington
Finished quilt size: 54" x 54" ■ Finished block size: 9" x 9"

Block Construction

Before you begin, refer to the instructions for pressing on page 11.

Friendship Star Block

1. Place 3⅞" squares of brown and deep gold fabrics right sides together. Draw a diagonal line from corner to corner on the wrong side of the lighter fabric.

2. Sew a scant ¼" from each side of the line. Cut apart on the marked line to yield two matching triangle squares. Repeat with the remaining 3⅞" squares to yield four triangle squares.

Stitch.   Cut.   Triangle Square
                               Make 4.

3. Lay out the triangle squares, four 3½" deep gold squares, and one 3½" brown square according to the block diagram. Sew the pieces together in rows and press the seam allowances open. Then sew the rows together and press in the same manner to complete one Friendship Star block.

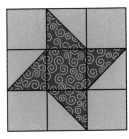

Friendship Star Block
Make 1.

Star Points Blocks

1. Place the 10¼" squares of deep rust and medium-scale floral print right sides together. Mark a diagonal line from corner to corner on the wrong side of the lightest fabric. Stitch on either side of the line and then cut the resulting triangle squares apart on the marked line, as described in step 2 of Friendship Star block above. You will have two triangle squares.

Make 2.

2. Place a triangle square and a 9⅞" deep rust square right sides together. Make sure the wrong side of the pieced unit is facing you. Draw a diagonal line from corner to corner *in the opposite direction of the seam that is already sewn.* Stitch a scant ¼" from each side of the line and cut the unit apart on the drawn line. Repeat with the remaining triangle square and deep rust square to yield four Star Points blocks.

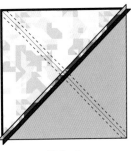 

Make 2.   Star Points Block
                 Make 4.

Half-Off Blocks

1. Place a 7½" green print square right sides together on one corner of a 9½" medium-scale floral print square. Mark a line from corner to corner on the back of the green print square, as shown. Sew on the line and then trim the excess fabric ¼" away from the seam. Press the seam allowance open. Repeat to make four Half-Off blocks.

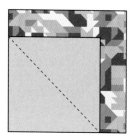

Half-Off Block
Make 4.

2. Repeat step 1 using 7½" medium-scale floral print squares and 9½" light gold squares. Make four of these Half-Off blocks.

Half-Off Block
Make 4.

 USING THE LEFTOVERS

You will have rather large pairs of triangles leftover from the Half-Off blocks. I like to sew these pairs together right away, creating triangle squares that I can use in another project.

Triangle Squares

1. Place the 9⅞" dark floral and light gold squares right sides together. Mark a diagonal line on the wrong side of the gold squares. Stitch ¼" away from each side of the line. Cut the squares apart on the marked line and press the seam allowances open. You will have eight large triangle squares.

Triangle Square
Make 8.

Quilt Assembly

See page 12 for instructions on assembling a straight-set quilt.

1. Arrange the blocks and background squares into five rows of five blocks each as shown, opposite. Sew the blocks together in horizontal rows and press the seam allowances open.

2. Sew the rows together and press.

3. Cut two of the medium-scale floral border strips in half and join a half strip to each of the remaining 4½" x 42" strips to yield four long border strips. See pages 12–13 for instructions on measuring and applying borders.

Finishing

1. Cut the backing fabric into two equal lengths and sew the pieces together to make a backing with a vertical seam. Press the seam allowance open. Trim the backing so that it is approximately 6" larger than the quilt top.

2. Layer the quilt top with the backing and batting; baste. Machine quilt as desired. A combination of free-motion and straight-line quilting enhances the stars in the quilt shown. The border is filled with a free-motion pattern of leaves and vines.

3. Trim the excess backing and batting even with the edges of the quilt top.

4. Use the 2½"-wide green print strips to bind your quilt. See pages 15–17 for basic binding instructions.

Quilt Plan

COLOR OPTION

A pretty floral and coordinating print fabrics combine in a summery version of Dawn's Star.

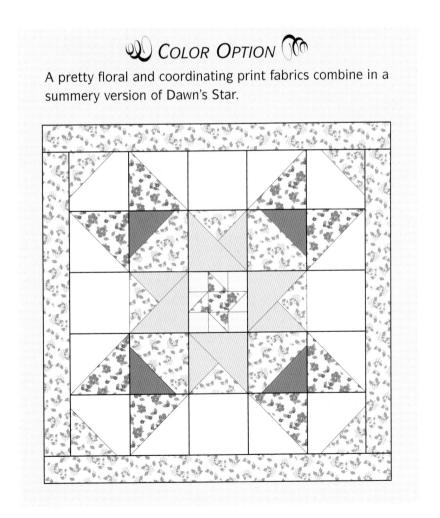

ABOUT THE AUTHOR

Beth Garretson has always enjoyed "making stuff" and started sewing at an early age. After stitching a queen-size medallion-style quilt completely by hand, the purchase of a really good sewing machine set her free! Many hours of hanging around her favorite quilt store resulted in a part-time job and the opportunity to teach classes. She enjoys seeing the proverbial light bulb go on over her students' heads and encourages them to drop the word "perfect" from their vocabularies. Every phase of the quilting process is fun for Beth as she alternates between traditional and contemporary designs.

Beth was born and raised in Everett, Washington. In 1978 she moved to Yakima, Washington, and fell in love with the wide blue skies, the sharp outlines of the surrounding hills, and the much lower humidity. She and her husband, Peter, share their home with a huge cat named Alix and their Welsh terrier, Gruffudd.